Finally Free!!

By

Nakisha Cole

Published by Jus King Publications

Chicago, IL.

Edited by Kita LaShaun

Cover design by Open Mic Production

Printed in the United States of America.

Contents

Acknowledgements

My life hasn't been perfect. In fact, it has been one hell of a ride. There are two sides of a track, the left side and the right side. If you are fortunate enough to reside on the right side, there may be a better education, a better support system, and more avenues for a brighter future, and safer streets. But cruising down my side of the track shows many difficult challenges, causing one to give up if not strong enough. The difference between those raised on my side of the track is they never believed that they could cross over. They never believed that there was life after the pain. Don't get me wrong. My side of the track was equipped only for the strong, but it was meant for survival. Only the weak wither and die. I have had some good days, and some bad. It seemed like most of my days were bad, but I had to go through life's trials to be able to speak to you today. I had to face challenges, meant to destroy me, so I can show people how strong my faith was. This book is dedicated to every person who told me "No," who told me I couldn't make it, and that I wasn't educated enough to make it. This book is for you. In life, we will encounter many people. Some will bless us and some will stress us. The only person that controls the engagement of your crossings is you. We deal with the same issues and the same people, expecting different results. Yes, it is true that people change. People think differently and will eventually start to act differently. However, you hold the safety key as to what gets deposited into your life. In this book, I will share some of my most inner secrets and feelings, and how I overcame them. I want to acknowledge God, who is the head of my life and who has taught me so many things about life and how to live it full of love and peace. He taught me how to change my thought pattern and how to love, unconditionally. I would like to acknowledge my father, who played a big role in my life, helping me become the woman I am today. His death helped mold me into who I've become. The lessons I learned at a very young age, yet didn't understand, were all because of his seasonal time in my life. To the many friends and associates I crossed paths with that taught me the true meaning of love and betrayal, to the lovers who caused my mind to be an emotional roller coaster...when I doubted my true self, you were there to either build me up or tear me down. I want to say thanks to you as well. I would not have been able to share my test and testimonies to the world and help someone else through their breakthrough. Last, but not least, thank you to my mother. You taught me so much about life and how to be independent while standing on my own two feet. The long nights and early mornings were not in vain, and you can see that everything that I've accomplished in my life was to make you happy. I hope this book helps you, the readers, as much as it has helped me to finally be free.

The Author

I am the CEO and founder of P.S.B.E. (Purpose-Driven Servants Believing Everyday), a non-profit organization that is geared to enriching, enhancing and empowering the lives of humanity. I am a mentor, communicator, and a motivational speaker at various events throughout the Houston Area. I have mentored battered women, as well as women going through temporary setbacks, and helped them all regain focus. My only objective is to give what God has blessed me with, and that is to be a leader to His people, to give aid when needed, and to help someone along the way. My objective is to continue to be the voice for those that are afraid to speak or cannot speak and allow others to shine their lights through my testimonies. I tell all of my mentees that in order to be someone successful, you have to come

from a place of trial, a place that challenges you to make a

difference.

➤ KNOWING YOUR WORTH

There may be times you are taken for granted because you are too nice. You try to fit in, or perhaps make someone like you. You settle for all the wrong things: that job where your earnings are just enough to get you by, or that relationship you stay stuck in because you're told that you won't find anyone else, or you're scared to walk away. You have gotten so comfortable, you'd rather stay than pray. What about the family members that are close, yet so distant? They speak to you only to get something from you, not even asking or worrying about your well-being. These are some of the signs of self-pity and self-agony, which causes self-pain. You don't know the person you are. More importantly, you don't realize the person that you can become, or the person you're destined to be. People use our scars and our past to try to control who we are. If not careful, they will assassinate who we are right now. Stop imprisoning your mind with the, "I can't," and, "I won't make it," mentality, because that is what the enemy is trying to convince you of. Look in the mirror and tell yourself that you are destined for greatness and you will not allow anyone to sabotage your yesterday, incriminate your present, or predict your future. Stand up, shake yourself off, and remember who you are. It is okay to have doubt or worry. We all worry. The most important thing is to recognize who you are. You can be with someone for many years, allowing that person to mistreat you. You may feel like you don't want to move on, or that you have invested too much time. Time won't make a person appreciate your worth, especially if they are mistreating you.

Walking away from time and showing your partner who you are, and what you will and will not allow, serves them proof that you know you're worthy.

Share an **experience** where you felt you were worth it.

_____

_____

_____

_____

_____

_____

_____

_____

_____

_____

_____

_____

_____

_____

_____

_____

Romans 12:2
Do not be conformed to this world, but be transformed by
the renewal of your mind, that by testing you may discern
what is the will of God, what is good and acceptable and
perfect

I was one of those people who didn't know who I was. I didn't know my worth, and only lived in the moment. I didn't allow myself to care about my significance because I was so focused on what everyone else's needs were, not even worrying about my own. I settled for what I knew and became content with being treated a certain way. It happened for years. I grew so accustomed to it, I didn't recognize who I was. I had to be broken down before I realized how important my life was to me. And, sometimes, that is what we need in order to know who we really are. As horrible as it may sound, no one wants to be broken down for fear of pain and instability. But, in some cases, it is absolutely necessary for growth and change that we all need. When you know who you are, a person will value you more.

If you are leery of who you are, you can't be upset with someone for not knowing your true worth. Your worth is based on how you value yourself. It's sad to say that sometimes we don't even know our worth, no matter how much we scream we do. Often times we don't. Then we wonder why we are treated a certain way.

What are some life lessons that you value now more than ever?

_____

_____

_____

_____

_____

_____

_____

_____

_____

_____

_____

_____

_____

_____

Philippians 3:13-14
Brothers, I do not consider myself to have taken hold of it.
But one thing I do: Forgetting what is behind and reaching
forward to what is ahead, I pursue as my goal the prize
promised by God's heavenly call in Christ Jesus.

➤ WHO'S FOR YOU

Let's talk about boats and why they are so important to us in our lives. A person that is not on the boat can be just as crucial to us as those on the boat. In order for the boat to sail correctly, everyone must be rowing in the same direction. You must ensure that every person in the boat is free from nails or anything that will prohibit or stop you from making it to your destination. Boats are important in knowing your worth because they signify who you are, who are you observing in your boat, and in your surroundings. It doesn't take years to realize that your boat is sinking, and it's okay to remove someone from it. In all honesty, you have somewhere you need to be. So, it is crucial that everyone in the boat is on one accord. Often times, we worry about those that are not in our boat because we can see they are not for us. Yet, we fail to even see that our boat is sinking from within. In life, we will meet these types of people who appear to have your best interests at heart. They appear to value you, your life, your dreams, and hopes. You pour so much in them without noticing that you are pouring much more out that you are pouring in. That business you are wanting to invest in but can never get it off the ground can be because the persons that you are attempting to share it with are not for you.

Who has been in your boat that should not have been?

_____

_____

_____

_____

_____

_____

_____

_____

_____

_____

_____

_____

I want to share a story about a friend whom I loved and cherished dearly. I thought that this friend would always have my best interests at heart, only to find out that person was only interested in the plan and not the planner. I was always naïve and a friendly person and would practically let anyone do whatever to me just to please them. There was this friend that I had known all my life. We shared secrets both professionally and personally and I treated her more like a sister. I always thought she was prettier than me because she was smaller. That was the first sign of insecurity and not knowing my worth. I wasn't jealous, but I definitely wasn't confident enough in me to compare with her, let alone anyone else. She needed me as a friend and I was there. I shared a lot of things with her, but the only thing that she seemed to care about at that moment was my plan.

My plan to be with who I was with and what I had going on

at the time. She betrayed me something awful and I still till

this day remember the smell from her garments. Without

going further into details, I (the planner) was forgotten about

and a temporary enjoyment costed her a lifetime worth of

loyalty. The ultimate was and the goal of anyone that wants

to heal is to let go. I did not want to let go, but it was

definitely needed to move forward with becoming a better

me, and knowing you I was. You have to ensure that the

people that you share your plan with genuinely care about

you. In order for any plan to work, there has to be a planner

who is positively able to construct the plan. You can't

construct it if you have people wanting to take your spot.

This analogy can be used in many ways, not just a way that shows someone trying to steal your dream. It can happen in friendships, families, marriages, schools, and on the job. You have to immediately find out who is for you and who isn't. Continuously build a team so strong that they will want to know your secrets and why you are still standing, despite the obstacles that you have encountered in your life. Sometimes, we often find that building a team is only designed for one or the other, friends or lovers, when in actuality it is designed for all. No matter what level you are at right now, you need to be sure that everyone claiming they're for you are truly for you. Life is too short to constantly be with people who don't add value to your life or who aren't wanting to see you happy. When you know someone means you well, you no longer get empty promises. You get commitment and dedication. You don't just get honesty. Honesty can mean, "Yea baby I love you, but I cheated with my ex." Although they were honest enough to tell you, you no longer get that. You get loyalty as well. With loyalty, they will take those temptations and push them to the side. See, hurting you is way more important than doing something without asking for permission, but confessing you did it after the fact. It is only through a person's loyalty that you can be trusted. A person that is for you will continue to show you they are for you and will show you how much they appreciate you. You certainly know who is for you when you go through your trials and tribulations. You can't mourn because they're mourning, you can't cry because they're crying, you can't be happy because they are not happy, you can't be in pain because they are in pain. Their only concern is them, never you. The one that you love, and that loves you, is not going to allow you to make them an option or give them boundaries.

Who is really for you?

_____

_____

_____

_____

_____

2 Peter: 2:21
For it had been better for them not to have known the way of righteousness, than, after they have known it, to turn from the holy commandment delivered unto them.

REAL LOVE DOESN'T HURT, IT HELPS

"For God so loved the world, that he gave his only Son, that whoever believes in him should not perish but have eternal life." John 3:16

One thing I've learned, dealing with love, is if you want something, you need to be truthful. Do not hide behind dishonesty because it hurts and can mess up a love that was destined to be. We all want love that lasts forever. We want the kind of love where lessons are taught, so they can see just how important we are to them. We desire that Cinderella type of love, or the hopeless romantic love...one that won't die. We yearn for the type of love that will prevail and one that has no flaws. Love is not about how much you can buy a person to manipulate them into being with you or even loving you. And love definitely doesn't hurt. So let's be honest , there is no such thing as a "perfect love", that is only a figment of our own imaginations, and that sometimes can have us being unrealistic at times. When we want the best love, but do not want to deal with the flaws. I am here to tell you that even the best of love has flaws. You may have to face some challenge, but the challenges you face make the love stronger. I've seen and experienced love on many levels including these that I am about to mention. One being a sweet love, only wanting to give and be accepted. This type of love doesn't hurt and it doesn't help either, if you are not mature enough to acknowledge it. A sweet love is one that is pure and has no intentions of benefits. Maybe the sweet love is just looking for love that will be there through good and bad times. If not careful, the sweet love will run away because they are not used to love and only want to receive feelings that they share. In other words, the sweetest love will be there to give you all of them and reject what you have to give. Then, there is hopeful love, the love that you attempt to build a family and make a future with, in hopes that things will be ok. This type of love is not promised because, although there is an understanding, there isn't a solid commitment for neither person. Both parties are needy and hope that the other can fulfill the desires they are looking for. We've heard it before when people attempt to go into relationships and only want to give 50%. Their favorite saying is " I want someone to give me half", or " I am only doing my half of this, or my half of that." But where is the real benefit. We should not want anything that is half. If a person can not give you their all or give you 100% then you should not want it. We should go into relationships giving our all. In some cases, even half milk doesn't fulfil a person that is desiring more. A hopeful love normally ends after a while because there is no faith. Someone will always feel like they have given more or they want more. You should always want a love that is given you 100. Then, there is the kindred spirits love. This love can be the love of all times, and perhaps a love that doesn't hurt, or at least doesn't hurt as much. Remember we said earlier that there is no such thing as a "perfect love". The spirits are connected together to form a solid bond that no one can break. It has to be the right time for this type of love to happen because both people need to be in a place where there is no worry and all peace. LOL, we can all pray that this happens. In fact, this is the best type of love experience it should happen in. A love of kindred spirits happens to be the most romantic of them all, and personally my favorite, because it shows acceptance. It shows that the person is not looking for anything other than knowing who you are, accepting who you are, and loving you for who you are. In any event the love of the kindred spirits part ways from one another, they will always have a special bond that will bring their hearts back to the very first moment of truth. If you ever encounter a love that is kindred, cherish it and hold it close to your heart. And lastly there is the toxic love. This love is one that means well, but it has been so contaminated that it doesn't give you a chance to love. It starts off as a sweet love but ends up toxic. In this type of love, you have to be sure not to put in more that you are receiving because you will definitely regret it. This is the type of love that will have you regretting there is love in the world, or perhaps that you can be loved. Toxic love is the most dangerous love there is and will hurt you. A person can be so toxic, unintentionally, that they damage and intoxicate you with feelings of doubt, self-pity, hurt, and shame. With toxic love, you may begin to do things that you don't normally do because you are scared to let go. You're scared of what may be said or what may be understood. A toxic love has a way of holding on after there is no more commitment. There is love out here for everyone. People with similar situations, ones who've faced issues, are NOT hard to love. When you shake yourself off, look in the mirror and FIX you, the right love will come to you when you need it to. It will not hurt. You have to be his/her biggest supporter so they won't have to confide in the world. Some people only want love, companionship, and security. When they don't get love, companionship, or security, they seek it in other people. We sometimes stay in situations because we are trying to be down, another word for loyal, or we don't want the person to think that we don't care about them or love them. Truth is, you will die trying to please someone who doesn't know how to treat himself/herself. Someone who loves you won't hurt you willingly. Hurt people do hurt people, and the sad part about it we allow it to happen over and over. People that love you will move mountains to ensure that you are okay and there is nothing hindering you from being happy. Waking up to someone every morning, knowing you both are happy, is all that really matters at the end of the day. The amount of money you two have won't matter as long as the love you share is true. Money comes and money goes, and that definitely doesn't make anything that is not solid, solid.

Have you ever thought that love hurts?

_____

_____

_____

_____

_____

_____

_____

_____

_____

_____

_____

_____

_____

John 4:1-21 Beloved, do not believe every spirit, but test
the spirits to see whether they are from God, for many false
prophets have gone out into the world. By this you know
the Spirit of God: every spirit that confesses that Jesus
Christ has come in the flesh is from God, and every spirit
that does not confess Jesus is not from God. This is the
spirit of the antichrist, which you heard was coming and
now is in the world already. Little children, you are from
God and have overcome them, for he who is in you is
greater than he who is in the world. They are from the
world; therefore they speak from the world, and the world
listens to them. ...

➡ HOW TO FIX THE CHEATING ISSUE

I know we have all heard the saying, "Once a cheater, always a cheater." Many people will say it isn't true because people change. That is true. People do change. This does not justify cheating. A cheater is someone of the past, and can be someone of the present if you allow it. It could be someone who may not be aware they are causing hurt to someone else. Or maybe it's someone who is afraid of being told"No." Perhaps, it is someone who is insecure with others' opinions. Here is how you fix the cheating issue. You leave them. You do not pass go. You do not try to repair a pattern that does not associate with total restoration. No one is perfect, I know. But you should not have to allow someone to do a practice run on you. We say it all the time... "But I love him. I love her." Love doesn't hurt, nor does it cheat. Cheating is like a thief; it comes to take something that doesn't belong to it. Cheaters will plot ways to take something that you worked so hard for. For years, we shape and mold our hearts and invest our time, peace, and joy into ourselves. Then here comes the cheater. Their biggest excuse is, "What you won't do someone else will." Well, if that is the case, then leave. Don't allow cheaters to continue to allow their selfish desires and ways cause you pain. Say to them, "If I can't be your all, then why ruin what peace and self-confidence I possess?" When we get cheated on, one of the first things we sometimes do is blame ourselves for not being so pretty, small, intelligent, or submissive...when in fact we can't control a person's behavior. So, if they chose

to step out and cheat, then that is on them.

Are you blaming yourself?

_____

_____

_____

_____

_____

_____

_____

_____

_____

_____

Never should we lower our standards or feel bad for being cheated on. Cheating doesn't necessarily have to be physical. It can be mental. In fact, I believe that emotional, or mental cheating is worse. The mind can torture the cheater and the victim for the current situation and for situations to come. Once a person is cheated on, he/she begin to have issues with trust. Once the trust is gone in a relationship, it is almost impossible to come back from that mind frame. Constant reminders of things will torture you. The cheater will think it is okay, if they haven't been caught. In their selfish mind, they believe they did nothing wrong. It takes some people to be confronted before realizing their wrongdoings. And it is my absolute belief that a person is only going to do to you what you allow them to do. They will think you are only as strong as you show you are. Once someone comes in and has the ability to continuously hurt you over and over again and use you, then they will. You become an emotional game, if you continue to allow this. Emotional cheating is leading to heartbreak and heartache all across America. Some people cannot even get their day started without constant wondering if their loved one is doing something against them. It will cause sleepless nights and much agony. You may think it is okay to talk to your ex, one you're still friends with. So, instead of being upfront with your significant other, you hide the conversations in hopes that they won't find out. This could be harmless. Yet, the mere fact that you have to sneak and hide to do it just doesn't sit well. Speaking from experience, stress can kill and will leave you suffering when trying to keep up with a cheater. As stated before, many can change once they realize the pain or damage they've caused, while making an effort by doing everything that they can to fix it. It is up to you to decide if the sincerity is worth it. I am not saying continue to start over because someone has cheated on you. I am saying fix the repeated cheating issues with someone that has hurt you by running as fast as you can and never looking back.

Are you willing to run or continue repeating the cycle of emotional games?

_____

_____

_____

_____

_____

_____

_____

_____

_____

_____

_____

Psalm 139:14 I will give thanks to you because I have been so amazingly and miraculously made. Your works are miraculous, and my soul is fully aware of this.

➤ I AM YOUR GIRLFRIEND, NOT YOUR WIFE

It's no one's fault that we allow ourselves to be caught up or labeled "wifey" without the benefits. Yeah, people say you have to show them who you are or prove that you are wifey material, but a WIFE is someone who is committed or has made a commitment to love, honor and respect their husband. Women start off spoiling men because they want to be treated like a king. But men are treating women like someone random. Husbands get catered to and spoiled with submissiveness. They expect you to give them all the things they want and can't give you any of the things that you need. The title "wife" is something that should be respected and acknowledged. The only way to get those privileges from me is for you to remind me what I mean to you. I was once told I had to prove that I was wifey material, or the "wifey type". That is something you don't have to prove. Either you have it or you don't. It is definitely something that can't be bought or borrowed. In the bible, Ephesians 5:33, Paul says that the wife must respect her husband and love him as she loves herself, doing everything that is needed to ensure that she is honoring him. She is appreciating and acknowledging his place in her life and ensuring him that her commitment to him is sincere and genuine. I would say that this type of love is one that is humble and unconditional. I do, however, know that you have to go through the girlfriend stage or "pre-wife" stage, because it's not every day in America that men can wake up and pick his wife or have a wife picked for him.

That would be a great benefit if it was to happen. Lol!!!

Psalms 18:22 He who finds a wife finds what is good and receives favor from the LORD.

Have you been robbed of your title?

_____

_____

_____

_____

_____

_____

_____

_____

It takes time, loyalty, commitment, communication, and a lot of love for one to be married and remain married. If I do all the things that the wife does before becoming the wife, then why would he want to get married, when he is already getting everything he wants? There is no sense in committing or making a lifetime commitment to someone. It is true that an official marriage is a piece of paper which doesn't guarantee love commitments and all other things we assume will happen when the marriage takes place. However, when I am your wife, you have total access. When I am not, you have limited access. That is the problem with most of us; we assume that the way to a man's heart is through the bedroom and through his stomach. Some men may like that. In fact, they may love it. But, he will respect a woman who knows what she wants and is consistent in knowing. He will value someone who doesn't play games or acts a certain way to get what she wants. Some men want the wife benefits, but not make YOU the benefit. We have to learn that we are the benefit and we have to stop minimizing our true value because he looks good or because it feels right. We are all guilty of this and God knows I have had my share of lustful situationships. (yea that's my word, lol).. We need to realize in order for anyone to respect our wishes, we have to be willing to be 100% in. There is no more time to waste in relationships that are not geared nor equipped to be everlasting. We stay in relationships because we are hoping for the best, and sometimes the best that we seek and deserve does not come from the one we are awaiting it from.

I challenge you to make a list of all your relationships and put the years associated with it. Once you do this, write next to it if you were an "assumed" wife, or was it just for fun.

_____

_____

_____

_____

_____

_____

And for those of us needing more space...

_____

_____

_____

_____

_____

_____

_____

_____

_____

We have to make sure that what we put in the same that we

expect to get back. I know most people may say you should

go into relationships wanting to give and not receive from it.

And that is a great mentality for those that have no feelings or have never been hurt. But for most people, we need to be sure that what we give is what we receive. We do not believe in minimizing our qualities. We know that a good woman, or even a good man, is hard to come by. And if a woman possesses the qualities of a wife, then a man would only be a fool to pass it up. You may be labeled as a person that is "bougie" or someone who is "stuck up." You should prefer be called those things than dealing with someone who is not appreciative of your time or your qualities.

What qualities do you have to bring to the table that can get you the ring?

_____

_____

_____

_____

_____

_____

Whether you are in it for the long haul or in it temporarily, be in it because that is what you desire. Again, we should always remember to never allow anyone to minimize our qualities by making us accustomed to the way they want us. When someone is serious about you, and ready to take your relationship to another level, they will. There will be no if, ands, or buts about it. They will accept who you are and accept your values as their mate. Do not discount yourself.

Ephesians 5:33 However, each one of you also must love his wife as he loves himself, and the wife must respect her husband.

➤ HEALING AND KNOWING THAT IT IS OKAY

Healing is a process; too many times, we feel that healing comes quickly. In some cases, it can come quickly. But any wound, cut, or scrape will have to properly heal in order for it to go back to normal. That is the same thing we deal with when we go through these relationships. We don't want to be left alone looking dumb or crazy, so we hop into another relationship with someone carrying all that old hurt. It is okay to take time out for yourself and get familiarized with who you are, while processing what has actually happened. No one wants to be the fool, and sometimes as women, we seem to believe that the other person already had hurt planted in them that they needed to release. Some women are drawn to hurt because that is all they know. We cling to those people who've been hurt because we can relate to the pain, or we understand where they are coming from. Understanding where they come from can cause us to revisit the pain that we never took to the time to heal from. This is all too familiar, because in the end everyone just wants someone to love and to understand them. The only way to fully heal is to focus on you and what you have going on. Stop comparing your life to the life of others. What you see from the outside is only a figment of your imagination. You never know what a person is going through, so what you visually see sometimes is not how they feel on the inside. When you go through the process of healing, you will also learn that some people know what to do and say to cause you to be removed from the healing process. When you also go through the healing process, you have to eliminate yourself from people that are associated with what you are in the process of healing from. Sometimes, it may seem as though we are turning our backs on them. Nevertheless, in order for us to grow from those situations, we need to remove ourselves. We have to assure them that their actions won't get a reaction from you because we know that some people will use everything that caused you hurt and take it away from your healing process. They will try to get you to a place where you are wounded all over again.

What steps can you take to move from your past? What steps have you taken to move from your past?

_____

_____

_____

_____

_____

_____

_____

_____

_____

Making peace with your past doesn't mean you have to

continue to live in it. It simply means that you are grown

and old enough to understand that not everyone is supposed

to go where you are going. It is okay to let go. Some people are only in your life to get what they can get (temporary love, clothes, attention, and money). It is okay to venture away from the things that have caused you pain. Too often, we sympathize when we are the victim because of our good mind and our good heart. Not only are we setting ourselves up to be hurt again, often times we fall right back in the arms of the one that hurt us. It will not be an easy task to walk away from something that has hurt you or is hurting you. You have to take it day by day, and step by step, and things will all work out. There are other people that want to see you make it and see you prosper. They are looking at you and believing that you can come out of this and that your healing is a part of the plan. The only thing with healing is you have to believe that you are worthy to be healed ad believe that it will happen. Only in your time of healing will you begin to leave things that are not meant for you alone and focus on you. I assure you, once you are in a place of true peace and true purpose and can identify your pain and be strong enough to know you made it through, then your life will go on.

Going through the healing process is not only difficult for you, but it also difficult for the people that love and care for you. Write down the things that are wounded in your life that need to be healed.

_____

_____

_____

_____

➤ AUTOMATIC DEFENSE

Sometimes, brokenness can cause you to become bitter, automatically taking up for yourself because you're defensive. Constant reminders of someone who love to argue with you, because they are insecure about what they have going on, is annoying and very disturbing. A person that is used to continuous issues and arguments ALL THE TIME will not know any other way than to become defensive in everything they do or say. Not every relationship you go into has to be the same. However, if they are, you need to revisit the common denominator in these situations. Most times it may be you, but if you are dating someone who has always had an issue with being faithful to their mate, then they will not be faithful to you. If they always get into fights, or is abusive, then you may need to ensure that this person is not the abuser. Hurt people hurt people. That has been my saying for so long. In order to heal from the hurt, someone is going to have to take responsibility for their actions. You ever notice that you are always trying to prove a point to someone to show them that you are being truthful? That can go both ways. While you are the accuser, you can very well be the person that is to blame as well. A person will go on and on, accusing you of the very same thing that they are doing. Some don't like the heat, yet refuse to leave the kitchen. In other words, there is nothing wrong with them cheating, stepping out, or accusing you, because they feel what they are doing is right. Perhaps it is uncommon for them to be wrong because someone did the same thing to them. Sometimes, that automatic defense mode is in because they know they are guilty of the thing that they are doing. Being manipulative and playing mind games is something that a person does who is always defensive.

Being defensive in situations does not necessarily mean that you are guilty of something, but majority of the times it does. Have you ever been in a situation where the person that was continuously accusing you of something happened to be the one that was doing something? How did you handle that?

Arguments lead to fights and misunderstandings between people that are not mature enough to realize everyone is entitled to their own opinion and everyone is not out to hurt or to use you. Being so defensive all the time can sometimes cause more damage than good. If you are a defensive person, whose reason is because you cannot trust someone due to everything you went through, you'll eventually torture the person you are with by accusations. That can run off the person that may be for you. It goes with taking time out for yourself, so you will know and understand that everyone is not the same, no matter how many similarities people may possess. Everyone is different, and not out to get you. Being a person that is always in defense mode, or always making accusations, will interfere with your future plans which will cause issues with someone you really like. It is also not healthy and causes you stress, resulting in health issues down the line. You can be a person of good health and in shape, yet make poor decisions that can stress you out, causing all types of pain. We all want to live a normal life, and it is known that some people worry. Some worry more than others, while some have no reason to worry at all. Past relationships, and even friendships, can leave some ugly scars that may never heal. So, we take all that into consideration when we are approached by the next person or friend. I mentioned earlier that it takes time to heal wounds from our past, and there is no time limit or amount of time to go by where we can say we are completely over a situation. It is only suggested that you take your time and ensure that you are healthy enough to make great decisions for your future.

Stress is the #1 cause of heart attack in the United States, and if not controlled can be detrimental to your health. What ways are you taking to prevent stress from taking over your body?

_____

_____

_____

_____

What I've learned is if you forgive people for the hurt that they caused you, it will prevent less stress, thus resulting in a good night's sleep. Holding on to things that can cause you to be excessively defensive is not good for you. Some people will fault you for everything that has happened to them if you allow it. They get offended when you try to help and offended when you refrain from helping. It does not matter what you say or do, they will always hold some type of malice, jealousy, or hatred toward you. Some people don't want to see you happy because they aren't. They will say all day that they are happy. They pretend to pray about certain situations and people only to find out what's going on with them to use it to their advantage. Only a selfish person would mess up what they have to satisfy their desires.

Ecclesiastes 7:18 It is good to grasp the one and not let go of the other. Whoever fears God will avoid all extremes.

⟫⟫⟫➤ NO PAIN, NO GAIN

We all want to see different results and to be a part of the difference, but no one wants to make the changes and moves to get there. Change takes time, sacrifice, and sometimes pain. We may believe that it is the end of the world when we do have pain, but there is a lesson in everything that we do. Everything we encounter has to go through a process in order for there to be change. It's similar to a baby being born. We have to push out our situations and give birth to the things that may be beneficial to our lives. Let's take the birth of a child for example. There are many steps that happen before the baby is born. For instance, the mom has to carry the child for an extended period of time, and while carrying that child some women face many challenges. The baby may not like a certain type of food, the mom may get morning sickness, and there may even be changes in the way they look. There may be many changes that cause them pain leading up to the day of delivery. There is a sufficient amount of pain because they are about to birth something beautiful into this world. Nothing they went through could ever amount to the feeling that is perceived once the baby enters this world. This is similar to the pain that we go through in our everyday lives. We suffer through so much heartache and so much pain, holding it in until we are "forever pregnant". We are continuously holding on to something that will never get a chance to grow, never get a chance to flourish or blossom because we have gotten so used to the pain. We have become so used to feeling the way

we feel, so we stay "pregnant." Holding on to something that

causes you pain will eventually deter you from functioning

in a positive manner.

Ecclesiastes 2:22 What do people get for all the toil and anxious striving with which they labor under the sun? All their days their work is grief and pain; even at night their minds do not rest. This too is meaningless.

What are you "pregnant" with that is keeping you from

giving birth?

_____

_____

_____

As stated before, the only way to heal from pain is to go through it. In this book, I mention several times how to be efficient and how to make it through several stages of our life. This is your healing season and your healing time. Going through the pain is not a bad thing. If you look at it in a bad manner, then yes it will be. Whatever you do to help you cope with the pain doesn't take away from the fact that you have to go through it. We must go through it to see the end reward. "I give what I want and I want what I give" is a saying that I have repeated many times. It has a lot to do with going through the pain, or the motions. Sometimes, it will hurt to say no, or even to say yes. It will hurt to walk away, but how will we ever grow when we do not do go through the process? There may be a chance that you have to go through what you are going through to meet the one who should be in your life. How would you ever meet the person God has designed for you if you don't go through the rough ones and the ones that were meant to destroy you? See, the difference between meeting someone that will help you deal with the pain is understanding that you have pain in the first place. We walk into "situationships," believing we are the "perfect one" and the only person to blame for the madness is the next person. We hide behind masks and piles of trouble and pain, not even realizing that our gain will help us release the pain as long as we acknowledge that it exists. Some people hide from pain because it shows a sign of weakness to them. One may believe that if a person sees their weakness, they might take their strengths for granted. Pain doesn't always have to be physical. It can also be mental or emotional. It is known that emotional pain is just as crucial as physical pain, if not more. If you are dealing with someone that is physically causing you pain, I urge you to run as fast as you can. No one should have to go through that type of abuse. Emotional pain is something that takes time to heal from and come out of. I'll tell you this... if a person has gone through any type of emotional pain and spent time alone to heal, they will gain everything that was taken away from them. Spending time with someone, year after year, does not mean anything if there is no good in it.

Years together should be years of unconditional love, not conditional rants and conditional love. You can be married for 20 years and still don't receive the love that you will get in 20 minutes. In fact, when someone can mentally stimulate you, then you know you have gained a winner. We often do not credit ourselves enough when we go through things because we may feel we are not capable.

What can you do to birth your blessings rather than hold on to the pain?

_____

_____

_____

_____

_____

_____

_____

_____

Go through the fire, but come out as if you haven't been touched. Allow someone to pick you up where you fall and enter your world. There is a gain. The only thing wrong with dealing with someone that has been hurt and broken is that they won't give you a chance to prove to them you won't hurt them. So, they bring that lie, that betrayal to you, and expect you to be the superhero. There are some good people still left here in this world. The only disadvantage of not being with you is your own insecurities and you holding on to that pain. You can turn a good woman/man into someone else if you push them. Understand and realize that something good comes from the pain that we go through.

Your story may encourage someone who is going through the

same things. Even more so beneficial to you if you ever

encounter a situation like you have. Pain is for the believer

that is strong enough to go through and gain what needs to

be gained.

➤ HOW TO GET THE TRUST BACK?

You may want to rekindle some things that were torn down and you may figure that it can be done in the blink of an eye. It is possible, depending on the individual, but it is extremely difficult to assume that a person will automatically trust you quickly again. First, you will have to be involved in everything that he/she is doing to show them you are being attentive so they can gain your trust back, because if you don't someone else will. They are at the point where they have already been through enough with you, so if you want a second chance, you are going to have to come with it. They are already having a hard time trusting you; making them feel good is one of the first signs in getting the trust back. Secondly, tell them how important they are because there is always someone looking for the mate that you have that doesn't trust you. I don't think people realize this because once they gain part of the trust back, they start to lack and go back to their old ways and start doing the same things that got them where they were in the first place. One of the reasons a lot of people do not make it is because once they get comfortable they do just that. Thirdly, apologize if you are wrong. Taking responsibility does not mean that you are weak. It just means that you have no hidden secrets and agendas and you want them to feel secure in what you are telling them. Definitely don't apologize if you don't mean it because they will know when you are doing things to agree with what they want done. If you mean something, then stand by what you mean. Never make the person feel bad because you are trying to get on their good side or you want

to play the victim. Too often, once the mate has regained

some trust back, people go back and do the things that they

once did because they believe if they got away with it the first

time, there may be room for more mess-ups. It happens,

and we fall for it.

Psalm 37:3 Trust in the LORD and do good; dwell in the land and enjoy safe pasture.

How many times are you going to take them back?

_____

_____

_____

_____

_____

One thing that we do, yet aren't willing to admit, is take our partner back, but hold on to the fact they messed up in the first place. Not only does it cause your mate to go back to their old ways, it ties into the things that were discussed in the book earlier. When you let go, you really have to let go. If we know we cannot handle the things that caused us to lo se trust, we have no right taking someone back for retaliation. Someone is bound to get hurt. Let's just hope it doesn't fall back on you. Some other ways we can get the trust back is by communicating. Talking about things help you to understand what your mate is going through, and the lack of trust in regards to some things that you've said to them and what is happening now. If you don't trust each other enough to talk about your issues, then someone may end up walking out. If there is no trust in a relationship, friendship, partnership, or marriage, then you have NOTHING. Communication rules the nation, and once the trust is rebuilt, then communication will be better for all parties involved. Never give your partner a reason to not trust you or revert back to the things that caused the mistrust initially. Once the trust is gone, there may be some issues retaining it. To get something solid and something meaningful is to give one hundred percent. Never allow anyone from the outside to know what is going on in between you and your mate because most times people want to know what is going on to meet their selfish desires. You should handle your issues with your mate and never go seeking advice from the next person. Too often, that results in a door needing to be closed. Learn to communicate and talk to each other until the respect is gained. Take responsibilities for your own actions. Look in the mirror and recognize your own issues. Two people building a bond and gaining the trust back should rely only on one another. If one doesn't have something, they should make ways to get it together, not separately. Of course, there will be women and men there to try to sneak in and get in where they fit in, even going as far as making sure you are okay as long as you have constant communication with them. That is unfair to the person you are committed to or making a commitment to, and even more unfair to the person that would risk it all to ensure that you have what you are asking for. That person is not your mate. These people you continuously allow to know what is going on between you and your mate are going to be the reason you don't get your trust back in your relationship. So, when two strong people get together, there is no devil in hell to tear them apart.

What ways can you relate to where the trust was gained and lost at the same time? Have you been the one that had to show you can be trusted? How well did that go?

_____

_____

_____

_____

_____

_____

There is no secret key to making relationships work, and sometimes what works for some may or may not work for you. It is up to that person to be responsible and take responsibility for their relationship if they want to see it work. No one should be responsible in gaining your trust back. You should.

➤ TEMPORARY FIXES

If you are loyal to someone, then stay loyal to them. Don't let temptation take you to places that can jeopardize the purity of your bond. Temporary fixes are just that. Only a selfish person who has no desire to fulfill anything in its entirety would let a temporary fix desire their bond. Life and situations happen that make you regret ever meeting someone, but when you make a commitment to be someone's better half, that is a commitment that's not temporary. Temporary things change often, and once you allow the fix to be successful, it will ruin everything that you worked hard for. Temporary fixes lead to jealousy, rage, anger, insecurity and even death. Selfishness and sneakiness will allow you to mess on your mate. In most cases, if not caught, once you fulfil the temporary fix, you will see that it was not worth losing what you have at home. Once you jeopardize your permanent, then the temporary won't have anything to do with you. People with morals and values want people with morals and values. There is no such thing as a mistake when it comes to this. You can always decide to do what is right to continue on with your permanent fix. The enemy preys on the weak-minded when there is not a solid foundation. You shouldn't allow anyone to make you an option or treat you like a temporary fix. I learned a long time ago that if a person wants to be with you they will come, ready to give their all. Under no circumstances should you ever accept being #2 or #3. God has designed you to be #1. A queen should never allow herself to settle for a temporary fix. Stand up and adjust

your crown. Of course, some will say when you stand up for

yourself, and put your foot down, that you are not "real."

Perhaps, they may make false claims that you aren't even

down for them. You should always put yourself first, even if

the consequences are being alone from time to time. If

he/she loves you, then you'd never settle. Anyone who

claims to love you wouldn't let you. One problem with

temporary fixes, when it comes to catching your mate

cheating, is that your partner gets mad at the other women

and they approach them, when in fact the only issue is that

you addressed it. When you deal with dogs you will catch

fleas. The temporary fix will soon fade away, and at this time

it may be too late. There is a song called, "Piece of My Love", which is what we desire... a piece of something. Why can't

we get the whole thing? Do we not realize that "whole" is

where the love is?

Psalms 1:1-3 Blessed is the man who doesn't walk in the counsel of the wicked, Nor stand in the way of sinners, Nor sit in the seat of scoffers; But his delight is in the law of the LORD; On his law he meditates day and night. He will be like a tree planted by the streams of water, That brings forth its fruit in its season, Whose leaf also does not wither. Whatever he does shall prosper.

Do you believe that you deserve to get the "whole

thing"?

_____

_____

_____

_____

_____

➤ MOVING FORWARD

When you decide to not accept being an option, some people may say you are not there for them or you're not "down." Just know this is only a part of the process. See, for the ones that they love, this is true. But the ones they love will not accept being an option or being another chick. You have to decide who is in charge of your life. Will you live or will you continue to let someone dictate your next move? Some people will never speak to you, never like your pictures on social media, never admire your success, never give you a compliment or never appreciate you. These are the folks that you should stop accepting. Those are the ones with negative minds, emotions, and feelings. The continuous exposure to them will keep you toxic. The analogy here is if you don't water some plants, they won't grow. Something happens when it's not taken care of. The once beautiful plant becomes withered and will eventually die. The plant can always come back when it is touched and taken care of by the right hands. Apply that to your life. In order to grow beautifully, you need to take care of yourself, and only let those that help you grow to touch you. Be responsible for what you deposit in your life. Be sure that even you impact someone's life positively. Some people won't celebrate you because they don't have anything to celebrate for themselves. In order to move forward, you have to break through the thing that is continuously breaking you. If a person is not trying to help you heal, you need to remove them from your life. The real solution to moving forward is to live the rest of your days happy and making positive moves. Entertain less stress and never accept being anyone's #2. Know who you are and know your worth. Know what you bring to the table, and don't allow anyone to eat from it that hasn't deposited or brought anything to it. Spend more time with your family and the people that love you. The key to moving forward is to forgive everyone that has hurt and betrayed you. If not, it will slow down the process. Be strong with not having time or room in your life to continuously fuss, fight, and argue about things that are not going to change. Live. You have things to do and places to be. What the devil meant for bad, God will always turn it around for his glory and for his recognition. Don't think you are in this race alone or for no reason. Every level of your life will come with some difficulties that will equip you with how to handle the next level. Let nothing or no one enter your life without an attempt to deposit. Deposit positivity, deposit love, deposit hope, deposit success. Life is too short to be stressing over a job that will replace you, a lover that will cheat on you or abuse you, a family that will disown or don't support you, and friends that want to be you. They want to be you so bad, they stop at nothing to bring you down. Live your life with peace. You do not have to settle. I know sometimes we can be immune to certain situations because that is all we've been around as far as we can remember. But I assure you, there is hope. Leave that negative energy in the past. Find you something that will soothe your brain and take you to a place of peace. In my opinion, if peace had a name, I would name her *Water*. This is my place of moving forward, and what elevates me to move to the next level. Calming water is the beginning of a beautiful love story. Stay encouraged and motivated even if you have to be the one encouraging and motivating. Keep doing you and don't forget to smile.

What steps will you take to move forward?

_____

_____

_____

_____

_____

_____

Notes

Highlights

_____

_____

_____

_____

_____

_____

_____

_____

_____

_____

_____

_____

From Author, **Nakisha Cole**

I want to thank each of you for sowing seeds of love into a part of my life. I hope and pray that this book gives you some type of hope, while reassuring you that you are not in it alone. If you are investing in yourself or sharing this book as a gift for a friend who might need some positivity, please share this book. All across the world, we all face these types of things whether we notice them at first or we notice them later. Everything happens for a reason, and everything that was meant to tear you down will not prevail. Some of us have to be broken down so we can see the bigger picture. I hope that my book gives you a "That's confirmation" moment, so you can realize it was not all in vain. I wish nothing but love and peace upon you and your life. I pray that your next move will be better than your last move.

Stay Blessed~~Kisha

Stay tuned for my next book... "The Eyes Don't Lie"

"*The cold awaits the house of forgiveness and love every night. Two years anticipating the warmth of satisfaction and loyalty. Eyes have seen, but ears don't believe because a set of anything moves viciously sometimes in an urgency to cause havoc. You never beg for the right thing. You only accept the sure thing. Although most packages don't come sealed correctly, it's going to take the pilot that isn't afraid to lead and not follow others. Wasted time +negativity =failure. Only lesson learned in this love fiasco is to let people remain where they lay.*"

www.ingramcontent.com/pod-product-compliance
Lightning Source LLC
Chambersburg PA
CBHW060954040426
42445CB00011B/1146